The Reinvention of Me

A Journey Of Self-Discovery

In A Disenchanted World

By Donna Anne Pace

First Edition March 2018

Second Edition April 2020

To receive signed copies of this book
from the Author, please email:
dpace547@gmail.com

ISBN: 9781673620368

Dedicated to my beloved children.
Thank you for being my pillar of support when all felt lost.

INTRODUCTION

Hello! Well, where do I start with this introduction? I guess the whole idea of writing this book on self-discovery was born out of an amazing trip that I took to New York City in January 2017 for my birthday. After all the trials and tribulations throughout my life, there came a time when I had the money and opportunity to do something that I had always wanted to do. At last, I was finally able to tick one thing off my bucket list! Just me and my suitcase taking a 3-day trip to one of the biggest cities in the world! Yep, there I was, a fully grown 'Kevin McCallister', with my woolly hat and scarf, walking around the streets of Manhattan all alone, and only occasionally lost! Besides bringing my 6 children into this world, going to NYC was an experience in my life that I will never forget.

But as life goes, not all experiences are easily embraced or accepted. By this statement, I mean coping with the one thing in your life that you never hope to ever experience - the loss of one of your children. It's with a very heavy heart that I type these words about my beloved late son Jamie who tragically succumbed to his illness of Acute Myeloid Leukemia in December 2010 at the tender age of 12. There are no words to ever express the hurt, pain, anguish, and sense of loss when you spend one day in your life burying one of your own children. A child that you carried for nine months, nurtured, loved, and endured such excruciating pain with to bring into the world. Yet the pain and tears of joy become a bitter symmetry when that pain turns into tears from a broken heart.

The equilibrium of life itself is thrown into disarray and defies the natural order of things. So how does anyone recover and restart their lives after enduring such trauma? Something so unprecedented, that it is too difficult to comprehend? Then, and only then, does anyone really come to realise the fragility of life and discover how courageous and strong they really are.

So here my story starts to unfold, like an origami duck, that has been created from a single piece of paper and uniquely contorted and transformed into a shape. Not just any shape, but a shape that has recognisable traits that define what it is. A single piece of paper full of carefully placed folds, crafted by human hands, which bring the paper to life. For isn't that what our life journey is about? Evolving. Metamorphosing. Learning. Creating. Loving.

Not one human being ever asked to be brought into this world, yet here we all are trying to figure out what our purpose is? Why are we here? By far, the most profound and fundamental question anyone will ever ask themselves, or another human being. From the moment of conception, when 23 maternal chromosomes and 23 paternal chromosomes fuse together, just like a matchbox and matchstick – a chemical reaction occurs creating a new element. When the sperm and egg fuse together (gamete), a burst of zinc radiates from the egg. This magical moment defines the incredible spectacle when a new life begins.

Our journey into the unknown began with a magical burst of light, yet we remained in darkness for 9 months. Fate then decided upon which month, day and time we were to be delivered through the birth canal and into a mysterious, secret, untold world that was to become our life on earth. My life began with a magical burst of zinc - a human life in the making - a time when we are growing and being prepared for the outside world. We have no prior knowledge of our fate or the environment we are to be born into. Our journey into the unknown begins here.

* * * * * *

Just a little note from me. I decided to write this book as it was something that I have wanted to do for many years. I believe that what we put out there in the Universe comes back to us. We all succumb to various dilemmas throughout our lifetime and it is a test of how strong we truly are, both mentally and physically. When we are born we have no knowing of what life will deliver to us on our journey. It is the unexpected wealth of surprises that shape and mold us into who we are right now, or who we choose to become.

Even though this book is very open, blunt, and sensitive, it is also equally upbeat, honest, and hopefully inspiring. For that is the whole purpose of writing it. I want to share my life with the world in the hope that it invites courage, positivity, inspiration, and also self-belief. I do not believe it is right or fair for anyone to be suffering in silence, to feel that they are not worthy or important enough to have their voice heard.

I have decided to include an interactive page at the end of each chapter for you. I have done this to give you the opportunity to write down your immediate thoughts, emotions, and feelings. I think that, sub-consciously, you will be ruminating over events in your own life, so what better time to try to find answers/solutions to your own problems, than when you are experiencing that rawness of reading a true story about another human being.

I have written this book, not only to try to heal my own wounds, but also the wounds of others. You will take your first step into my life from a tender age as I unravel the mental scars that are yet to heal. This is not a 'tale of woe', but yet, a tale of one woman's journey to overcome a psychological mountain - one that is exhausting to climb, and yet without a peak.

A little bit about my educational background. I am currently studying for a BSc Health Science Degree and have thoroughly enjoyed completing the following Modules:

- Human Genetics & Health Issues
- Molecules, Medicine & Drugs
- Human Nutrition
- The Empire of the Microbes
- Elements of Forensic Science

Short courses

1. Forensic Psychology

2. Forensic Science and the Criminal Justice System

3. 2-day Life Coaching Workshop (UK)

4. Parenting Skills - 12 weeks

5. Pattern Changing - (Domestic Violence & Cycle of Abuse)

6. Certificate in Moving & Handling Practical Training

7. Certificate in Medication Practical Training

8. Certificate of Attendance for Dignity Workshop

9. Certificate in First Aid for Children & Adults

10. Life Coaching: The Integrative Wellness Model

11. Alumni EmpowerU Masterclass USA

MY A-Z OF SELF-DISCOVERY

Abuse

Bereavement

Counselling

Devotion

Emotions

Fear

Gratitude

Heartache

Isolation

Joy

Keyboard

Loneliness

Magazine

News interviews

Opportunities

Perseverance

Questions

Radio

Sacrifice

T.V.

Understanding

Violation

Waldorf Astoria Hotel

XX / XY

Yearning

Zinc

CONTENTS

Introduction

My A-Z of Self-Discovery

Chapter 1 – Alpha & Omega

Chapter 2 – Believe in Change

Chapter 3 – The Price of Bravery

Chapter 4 – It's All In The Mind

Chapter 5 – What Am I Worth?

Chapter 6 – Gratitude

Chapter 7 – New York City Baby!

Chapter 8 – Love & Laughter

Chapter 9 – The Art of Bonding

The Reinvention of Me

CHAPTER 1
ALPHA & OMEGA - AΩ

'PUSH…PUSH, THAT'S IT, KEEP BREATHING. The next time you get a contraction, push down deep into your bottom, the head is out, nearly there'! 'Aarrrgghh', went my mum with such ferocity and strength, pushing as hard as she could to bring me into the world. 'That's it, push push push, the head is out, one more push come on'. 'Arrgghhh, oh my goodness, oh my goodness.' It was at that point in January 1972 that I made my journey from the darkness into the light. Little did I know at that time, well, how could I, that my parents would be handing me over to my mum's Doctor and his wife for them to look after me for the first two weeks of my precious life. There was to be no celebrations when I arrived home from my older sister and older brother to greet me, cuddle me, or kiss me. There was to be no mother-and-daughter bonding - the smell of my mother's skin against my little nose. The first taste of my mother's milk which would have provided me with not only the nutrients I needed for growth and development, but also lots of precious antibodies (Immunoglobulin IgA). IgA would have enabled my tiny little body to absorb and digest my mother's milk to help build immunity from the harsh environment of the new atmosphere I was born into.

Daily life at the time of my birth was very difficult

for my parents. My mum had mental health issues and was an alcoholic, and my dad was doing everything in his power to keep the family together, to protect us all from harm. I have no ill feelings about being 'giving away' for a couple weeks after I was born. I was not walking in my parents' shoes, so I have no idea how difficult their decision was, or how emotionally distraught they were. As a parent myself, I can only imagine how traumatic that decision must have been for them both. My mum needed psychiatric help and my dad was working long hours to provide for us all. Becoming a parent is the hardest job in the world, and when faced with extremely difficult circumstances, you have to think fast, and act accordingly. I love my mum and dad very much. Yes, as you will now go on to read, my childhood was traumatic, and if I could turn back the clock to change my experiences I would. But would I now be the same person that has typed these words, probably not? Our own life experiences shape and define us into the human beings we are today. Take comfort in knowing that your past was your past; you are in the present moment right now; and your future will evolve by accepting both.

* * * * * *

Mum, why didn't I go to school today? Can you take me please? 'No Donna, you're staying home with me, I need you here with me'. 'Do you love me Donna, do you love me?'. Erm, yes of course mum. 'Ok, come with me', my mum said. Where are we going mum, what you gonna do? 'Just come with me'.

My mum took my hand and walked me to the bathroom, a cold, silent, fearful walk I took many times a week, a month, a year. Who could I cry out to? Who would save me from the horrors of what I was about to witness, and not for the first time. I was only 5 years old and yet my mind felt like it was maturing at an advanced rate, beyond the realms of what a childhood should be about or how it should feel.

My mum was drunk, as usual, and knew that with no one in the house, I was not about to run off in to the arms of my dad or siblings to seek comfort or refuge. Neither was I going to scream out for help, after all, who would hear the haunting screams of a 5 year old girl?

My mum picked me up under my arms and sat me down on the edge of the bath, before she walked over to the other end of the bath to perform an act of self-harm that I was sadly all too familiar with. I sat with dread in my heart thinking that the silver, sharp razor blade that she was holding in her left hand would be the tool of my demise. That I was going to die at the hands of my mum after being slashed continually across my body.

These harrowing thoughts should never be a part of any child's thought processes. No child should have to suffer that kind of psychological abuse, at any age. Instead, my mum grabbed the razor blade in her hand and proceeded to slice and slash her wrists, deep red blood trickling from her arms on to her clothes and on to the bathroom floor like a punctured carton of milk. My mum's demeanour was strange, as if it wasn't her in the room, but the soul of someone else, someone sinister, emotionless and cold. How could this woman sitting in the bathroom with me, be subjecting herself and me to such trauma, and yet she carried me for 9 months and brought me into this world? Where are the maternal instincts? Where's the sense of love and protection that any mother would provide for their young?

I sat terrified on the edge of the bath just wanting to run to the door and out of the house. I never knew where I was going to run to, just run. I was a quiet, timid child and my mum used this to her own advantage. I was kept from school many times as my mum knew I was never going to tell anyone – not my dad or siblings, what she was subjecting me to every week. I knew in my heart that if I ever told anyone, she had the potential to take my life, and at the tender age of 5 years old, I was not prepared for that, not mentally or physically.

My mum used to cover up her arms and wear clothing that hid the physical scars from all the family, yet I had to bear the brunt of the mental scars that were invisible to all. Everyone just thought I was a quiet, shy child that always refrained from getting into any conflict or arguments with anyone. Little did they know the reasons for my quiet nature and why I was so very scared to speak up for myself. The sofa in our home proved to be a good hiding place for me when my siblings were home from school and my dad home from work.

I needed to seek refuge somewhere out of the way from everyone so that any eye contact with any family member was limited. The eyes are the window to the soul and I knew at the age of 5, that if my eyes depicted the horrors of what I was being subjected to, my wrists would be the next to succumb to the silver razor blade that had become one of my mum's best friends.

The feeling and sense of relief when my 3 siblings returned home from school was indescribable. The thought that I was going to see them again and live to see another day gave me hope that perhaps one day my life may change for the better, and someone might come to realise my mum's daily routine.

Drawing heals my soul, even if it depicts the darkness.

But from the darkness we discover our hidden light.

Due to the fact that my mum had a way of hiding her physical scars so that no one noticed them, this tactic gave her both time and opportunity to continue to do the things she was doing. My mum warned me that if I told anyone, she would kill me. At such an innocent age, this thought filled me with intense fear and insecurity. I didn't want to die so young, I wanted to continue to see my dad and siblings. To go to school, play in the park, and see my next birthday, Christmas etc. I didn't want the mental images in my head on a daily basis of a scenario where my mum would keep me from school one day to use me as 'her wrist' and re-enact the 'bathroom scene', but this time, the end result being my very own demise.

When my dad returned home from work every day I think he knew exactly where I was going to be. It became routine and my dad would come to find me hiding behind the sofa. I obviously couldn't' tell him anything, how could I knowing what the repercussions would be! My dad comforted me and gave me a hug and asked about my day. All I can remember ever telling him was that I had fun at school and I missed him whilst he was at work. My older siblings weren't aware of the psychological abuse that I was being subjected to. My twin sister was kept from school sometimes and endured the same horrors as me. But unfortunately, my mum seemed to have a 'soft spot' for me, so I ended up remaining at home most of the time. Why did my mum have a favourite child? What was so special about me? Why was mum keeping me home with her so often, and not one of her other children?

The reason lies in age and personality. My twin sister and I were very young, but my twin was head strong and outspoken, so my mum played a tactical game and I guess my twin and I were like chess pieces. I was the Pawn and my twin was the Queen. My mum was mentally unwell but she knew how to play a psychological game. If she had chosen my twin instead of me, it would have been 'checkmate'.

The days that I went to school were such a relief to me. The thought that I was going to be in a building, a safe environment, with adults and children that I thought could be my protective blanket. I could see my friends, run around in the playground, paint pictures, and go to the toilet without the fear of my mum constantly watching over me.

Well, that's what I thought. On a daily basis, I never knew from one day to the next what was going to be instore for me. Was my mum going to take me to school with my twin sister, or was I going to be counting down the hours to my possible demise? On some occasions my mum would let me go to school but would then eventually end up barging her way into the classroom, arguing with the Headteacher and teachers. My mum would insist on taking me home. I remember one time when I was around 8 years old, when I saw my mum's face up against the glass of the classroom door, with the look of anger in her eyes. I knew that she was there to drag me out of school, take me home, and make me witness yet another 'slashing of her wrists'.

I am not embarrassed to say that on this particular day, whilst sitting on my grey chair, in a circle with my school friends in the classroom, I took one look at my mum and literally wet myself. Yep, the sheer fear and insecurity of seeing my mum's face through the glass prompted an emotional and physical response from me, and I was so upset. I don't remember anyone laughing at me, and my teacher did not want to let me leave the classroom. But my mum was head-strong and was definitely not leaving without me!

My mum had serious mental health problems and the fact that alcohol became her 'best friend' did not bode well with my dad. How on earth was my dad supposed to work all the hours he could in order to put a roof over our heads and food on the table, when it became apparent that his wife was becoming an alcoholic and her mental health was erratic. 'No man is an island', and that included my dad. I remember many times when my dad would come home from work exhausted and hungry, yet there would be no dinner waiting for him.

My mum was too busy getting drunk and abandoning her own children. The force and power that a bottle or can of liquid can have is truly shocking. How could my own mum choose the contents of a bottle of wine or Vodka over her own children? I was obviously far too young and innocent to form any constructive answers to this question, yet it plagued me that our well-being wasn't important as - where my mum's next drink was coming from?

My dad felt torn up inside knowing that without him going to work we would end up on the streets, yet, at the same time, by leaving us in the care of our mum we were at risk of verbal and physical abuse. When was this nightmare going to end? How was it going to end? Would my mum finally take her own life, like she kept telling me every day, or would she take one of her kids with her? Daily life became a struggle for everyone, all living in fear because of one person. The dynamics of our family became unsettled, emotional, mentally challenging, and erratic as we adjusted to the harsh realities of what daily life was morphing into for all of us.

I have lost count how many times my mum smashed up the houses we lived in. Smashing windows, ornaments, threatening to kill herself. I remember one evening when my mum was drunk and lost her temper with us all and she proceeded to verbally abuse my dad and us kids whilst smashing the living room windows and threatening to hurt my dad.

I remember the Police turning up, of which felt like an eternity. We were all terrified, not just because we didn't know what was going to happen to our mum, but because we didn't know if she was going to treat us in the same way as one of the living room windows?

The Police Officers charged through out front door to detain my mum and arrest her for damages to the property and for threatening behaviour, not just towards her husband and kids, but towards the Police Officers. I knew my mum was not going to go quietly or without a fight, and I can recall one of the Officers hitting my mum over the head with a truncheon in self-defence. My mum was 5'9" and with a slim build, but her feisty, drunken demeanour proved challenging that particular night.

That night was just one of many nights, and days, of incidents where my mum lost total control of her actions. My dad's health was suffering and he started to randomly pass out. We would rush to our dad's side to comfort him and wake him up. The mental anguish that was taking over his mind and body was too much to bear. Our family unit was crumbling and so was our state of minds.

The emotional trauma of witnessing the incidents I did throughout my childhood still haunt me today. In my 20's I thought that I would be able to put my childhood into the 'emotional dustbin' and learn how to come to terms with the dysfunctional family unit that I was born into. But how does anyone ever come to terms with such debilitating psychological abuse?

Irrespective of how much CBT (cognitive behavioural therapy), life coaching, or emotional support you receive throughout your life, I don't personally believe that the demons are ever fully destroyed. But that is my opinion and appreciate that not everyone will agree with me. After all, we all have our own ways of dealing with the day-to-day stresses of life and there are a myriad of tools and resources that we can make available to ourselves to help us repair what is broken.

I was foolish, I guess, to think that life would become easier once I got married and started a family. What I mean by easier is the fact that I was slowly finding ways to manage the psychological trauma in my head in order to create and live a 'normal' life. But how do we define 'normal', as we all have our own perception of what we deem it to be.

In my early 20's I got married and settled down with someone I thought was the 'man of my dreams', 'my saviour', after all the abuse from my childhood and adolescent years. Yet, unfortunately, time was to unravel the true nature of the man I married and the family I married into. Why did I gravitate to such a controlling, manipulative, possessive man? Was it because the behavioural traits were not uncommon to me? Perhaps I thought I had the power to help my husband come to terms with the negative elements of his personality so that we could embrace the issues we had between us and find common ground with which to create a happy marriage? But did I have the right to change the man I married and vice versa?

At what point do you draw the line in a relationship and let your partner know that their behaviour is unacceptable and abusive? How does anyone approach such a sensitive and volatile subject? After all, due to my past, I was well experienced and knowledgeable enough to realise that speaking up could incur serious repercussions.

My marital life was to become embroiled and entangled with abuse – abuse that took on many different forms, and there I was again, in an environment where someone thought they could manipulate, control, instil fear, dictate, frighten me, in order to get what they wanted and get me to live my life on their terms. How did I end up in that situation for 20 years? Why on earth did I let myself become half the woman I used to be? Why do people think that their actions are 'normal' and 'acceptable' and that there are no repercussions for what they have put you through? Perhaps those individuals who choose to mentally or physically abuse the ones they love is a way of coming to terms with their own life experiences? Maybe some individuals have witnessed abuse in their own homes and do not know how to deal with such pain and trauma and so go on to abuse others?

My in-laws were controlling and very possessive of their son. Is this why he treated me the way he did then in our marriage? Did he feel that trying to take control of his life meant trying to control mine? Instilling the very same emotional trauma onto me? No one is perfect in this world and there are some situations, incidents or behaviours that we can accept in our lives. But at what point do we say, 'enough is enough'?

So, there it is – my childhood, adolescence and married life ending up being contorted and molded into one big abusive world. A world which sadly was not alien to me, and yet very debilitating and destructive.

How far can one human being be pushed before they break their silence?

The Invisible Darkness

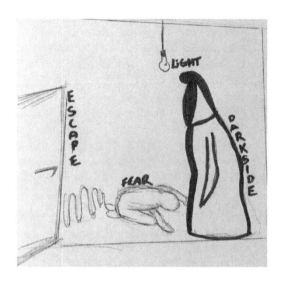

Walking down the stairs filled with fear and dread

Will I make it past the bedroom or will I end up dead?

What is this overpowering invisible darkness luring me into the room?

I'm too terrified to speak, to look up at the impending doom

Can someone save me from the man who floats gently in the night

I'm terrified he will make me look up at him

Is anybody there? Please switch on the light.

NEW BEGINNINGS IN MY LIFE

NEW ENDINGS

CHAPTER 2
BELIEVE IN CHANGE

My Personal Journey:
the re-invention of me!

So, WHERE DO I START? I have endured many life experiences since the tender age of 5. Growing up in a large family unit was fun but at the same time quite difficult. Sibling rivalry is a tough element to deal with, especially when you have a twin. Going through my adolescent years was a whirlwind of emotions from how I was being brought up to how my peers were treating me at school. By this I mean cruel and spiteful behaviour. I have Mediterranean heritage and racism played a big part in the school playground. I can remember the other kids at my primary school calling my father 'a black b!!!!!d', and that we should 'all go back to where we came from'! I used to reply to those remarks with, 'go back home?... well, I only live just 10 minutes down the road'! The comments were hurtful and use to upset me.

The kids at school didn't know my dad, didn't know anything about my family, yet they judged him, and us, on the colour of his skin. How ignorant can people be? The abuse didn't stop there, oh no! Coming from a large family with very little money, I didn't have the nicest clothes, shoes, etc. and the kids at my school made a point of bullying me about that. I used to ignore their comments and just go along and agree with them. By responding in this way, I knew it would annoy them as they were always looking for a fight. I always told myself to not lower myself to their standards and to just carry on with whatever I was doing.

I was born and brought up in South East London within a multi-cultural community. Even though I lived in London, my upbringing was very much Mediterranean – strict and controlled. To some degree, I guess I was glad that I was brought up this way, but it had its downsides. To not have the flexibility or freedom to have sleepovers, or friends' round, or very rarely be allowed to socialise with friends, affected how I interacted on a social level and it took me time over the years to build up my confidence, especially with talking to boys.

Throughout my time at secondary school and college the impact of my upbringing became recognisable to other students, especially the male ones! They would engage in banter with me that I did not understand and which made me blush! I guess I can only describe myself at that time as a 'lamb to the slaughter'. It was evident from my personality that I was a very shy, and not a very confident young lady, who was neither very knowledgeable when it came to 'dating' and all that went with it! When I think back about it now, I giggle to myself at how naïve and vulnerable I must have looked!

From the moment I left college and entered into my first job, for once I actually started to feel like a grown-up – a more confident, chatty woman who was finally breaking down the walls of my shy, timid personality in order to let the 'inner me' shine.

Since 1990 to present day I have worked in many different industries – property; advertising (where I met some wonderful people, some of whom I am still good friends with today); financial; retail; health & social care. I found that being in employment gave me a huge boost and I realised that I was blossoming into an educated, smart, intelligent woman who had control of her own life. I had the power to decide whether I wanted to go out for a drink with friends or not, what clothes I wanted to wear, how long I stayed out for, who I dated, etc. Yet in the back of my mind, there was always that sense of having to 'ask my family for permission'; 'to justify my decisions', 'to explain my actions'.

It is down to the fact that due to the disgraceful behaviour of some members of my own family over these past few years towards me, that I no longer think this way and have defended myself as and when needed.

Some families choose a 'scapegoat' within the family unit, for whatever reason, and unfortunately, since childhood, I was that scapegoat. But in 2014 I said 'enough is enough' and started speaking up for myself and disagreeing with the actions of my family members. As you can imagine, my opinions were not appreciated and my family made their thoughts and views very clear to me – in a manner of which was very abusive and controlling.

In 2014, I took the courage to finally walk away from my marriage, after a turbulent and traumatic 20 years. Yet again, without realising, I entered into a relationship which was just like my upbringing – controlling, manipulative, abusive and debilitating. At what point in any relationship do you make your voice heard and explain to your loved one that their behaviour towards you is very unhealthy and perverse?

My husband said he loved me – but is love about controlling and manipulating the person you married? Why do people seek to change the person they married into someone else? Surely, the traits of the person you married are the very same reasons as to why you fell in love with them in the first place? I thought I loved my husband and he loved me, but during our 20 years together, traits of our personalities surfaced and it became evident that we were actually poles apart. No one is perfect and we all make mistakes throughout our life – some minor, some major. Most of us humans try to be the best that we can be and have some degree of compassion, understanding and empathy.

After years of working in different employment sectors and meeting lots of people, I was gradually morphing into the woman I wanted to be. But sadly, it slowly became apparent that my marriage was not all what it seemed to other people, or to me, and my 'brave inner self' was slowly deflating. The words, actions, and demeanour of my husband became very volatile and abusive. I made a gradual progression to start 'walking on egg shells', 24 hours a day, 7 days a week. I didn't know how to cope with how I was being spoken to and treated. How would you define 'harassment' and 'stalking'? How can anyone cope with these issues, in any area of their life? What happened to the man I married? Who was this manipulative monster that he was evolving into? Why did he think that stalking me around the house, on my phone, and at work was 'normal'?

Can you imagine what it feels like to live in fear from morning to night? To wake up knowing that the man I married was going to follow me around our home, and do things like stand behind the bathroom door whilst I am in the bath (of which I was always too scared to tell him that I was having a bath). I was terrified to tell him 'no' as I knew the repercussions – he would become agitated and refuse to talk to me or kiss me goodnight at bedtime. He would become irate and abusive, and I always felt like I was to blame.

In order to keep the peace and protect my children from the wrath of his temper, more often than not, I use to do what he asked of me. I was scared in my own home! Daily life would encompass my husband following me around from one room to another, like one of our children. Whenever I was on the telephone, he would follow me and listen in on my conversation. He would go through my handbag, read my diary, or even go through my purse. Again, I was too scared to tell him that his actions were wrong. Sometimes I did tell him and his response was always the same – negative. Being someone's partner does not entitle me or you to 'just help ourselves', or to put unnecessary pressure on to someone we love for our own gain, albeit sexual or not.

Throughout the 20 years I spent with my husband, the duration of time showed me that I had made a huge mistake and that I no longer wished to spend any more of my life with such an abusive man. Don't get me wrong, we did have nice times during our marriage, especially the birth of our children. But the quiet, funny, kind man I fell in love with completely changed once he put a wedding ring on my finger!

The things that I endured and the types of abuse I was subjected to has had a major impact on my mental and physical well-being. How can someone declare that they love you, yet put you through so much - even using your own children as emotional blackmail?

Trying to remain in employment was an uphill struggle as my husband was extremely jealous and possessive. He didn't even like my own father or brothers sitting next to me on our sofa. Work life became very stressful for me as my husband would harass me every day with countless telephone calls. He wanted to know how many men were in the office? What were their names? Do I have their numbers on my phone? Questioned the clothes I wore to work. Whilst I type these words I am full of disgust, anger, shame and hurt. To allow another human being to treat me that way. My husband wanted to get inside my head and know my every thought. This absolutely terrified me and juggling work/kids/marriage/my family, began to take its toll on my health.

I became very nervous, scared, fearful, exhausted, depressed and quiet. I was too scared to tell my husband whenever I had a work function to go to because I knew that in order to feel like I was 'allowed out', I needed to be 'the good wife' when I returned home. Yes, how degrading is that? I wasn't his wife, or mother of his children. I became a sexual object, and no matter how I was feeling from day to day, I don't think he cared, he just wanted his needs taken care of. I am sickened to my very soul at how inhumanely I was treated, and yet he lulled me into a false sense of security by getting me to believe that our married life was normal, and my reactions to it were not.

In the year 2000, a very serious incident occurred between me and my husband, one of which I remember telephoning two of my close family members about, around a week later. I can remember crying, stuttering on the phone, trying to tell them what happened to me and that I felt like it was my fault.

Both my family members reassured me that it was not my fault and said that my husband 'had issues that he needed to deal with'. Let's move along to 2014 when I reported the incident to the Metropolitan Police and gave a statement. In these scenarios, it was my word against his. My only saving grace at the time was for two of my family members to give a statement to the Met Police confirming what I had told them in the year 2000. To my absolute horror, both of them declined to back up what I had told them. I was, and still am absolutely heartbroken at their lack of empathy, understanding and intervention. I broke down in tears when a female police officer from the Met Police telephoned me in 2015 to explain this and inform me that no further action could be taken due to lack of evidence. Why they both made this decision will never make sense to me? All I can say is that, at that given time, they both acted in a way that they perceived as 'right' to them, but so wrong to me.

That day, and the days since have eaten away at me like a ravaged wolf consumes its prey. I was informed by the police officer that my family's decision to not intervene was because they didn't want to get my husband into trouble. From this point on, I started to receive text messages and phone calls from my father and siblings trying to tell me how to live my life! Some of them verbally abused me and told me that I am 'deranged', 'mentally ill', 'that my husband is a good man', 'that I don't deserve my children' and 'that I am scum of the earth', and 'that I was wrong to try and get my husband into trouble'.

At the end of 2015 I received a telephone call from a Police Officer to let me that know that one of my ex-husband's work colleagues had been asking personal questions about him, and then went on to inform me that I was not to talk to anyone about my ex-husband or my marriage. Yes, the audacity of it! Again, there I was being silenced by yet another individual. Wanting me to 'keep silent'! The Police Officer in question told me to not discuss my marriage with anyone at school or my ex-husband's work colleagues as it wouldn't be fair on him, especially if he ended up losing his job. Wowzers! I was absolutely shocked at what was being asked of me. No one has the right to tell someone what they can or cannot talk about to another human being! I broke down in tears on the phone – my family's behaviour, my ex-husband's behaviour, and now this. I just wanted to take my last breath and be with my beloved late-son Jamie.

I came to realise that some members of my family were of the same mindset as my husband – controlling, manipulative and abusive. I did not have to put up with their inhumane crap, neither did I have to keep them in my life. Therefore, I blocked them on social media and on my phone. How can one family impose such hostility, judgement and negativity onto their own flesh and blood?

As of December 2019, some of my close family members have made contact with me, and to my surprise, initiated communications to show love. I am finding it overwhelming, trying to heal emotional wounds. I am adamant though that I will continue to refuse to let people into my life that seek to cause me any pain. I have grown thicker skin, become more outspoken and more determined in my quest to live a better life and remain the person I am.

Since 2014, I have tried to remain emotionally and physically strong in order to deal with most of my family showing allegiance to the very same man that abused me for years. My family witnessed some degree of abuse throughout my marriage, yet when I took the brave step to speak up, a couple of family members said to me 'what abuse'? I have no say in who or why other people choose to remain friends with my ex-husband. It is their perogative whether they choose to socialise with him. Some members of my family may still choose to refrain from communicating with me, but I have come to terms with this and continue to live my life.

I face some degree of hostility at school; hearing negative comments about me as a person and as a mum; I have faced the threat of eviction; I have tried my hardest to cope with living without my children; to try come to terms with my mental and physical health problems. Believe me, this unnecessary accumulation of negatives has been, and is still difficult for me to comprehend. But on the positive side, I have become a lot braver, more head-strong and determined than I thought possible.

The Changing of the Tides

I was running my own small business in 2017 and thought I had made the right step in my life towards gainful employment. But as the months went by, I became depressed and found it a daily challenge to motivate myself. My heart wasn't really in it and that I wanted to use my time more creatively. Whilst pondering on my next challenge an unexpected yet equally amazing thing happened to me. I was reading a heart-wrenching story on Facebook about a young girl that needed proton therapy treatment abroad and her family were trying to raise funds. I decided to reach out and help this family by way of offering my time and support. I was in dialogue with a lady called Kate Batten and we chatted for ages about life in general. From that impromptu connection, my life was changed! It came to light that Kate Batten is a Publishing Specialist and has written many books.

I decided to put my creative skills to work and wrote a 'parenting story' about my eldest child. I submitted it to Kate and she loved it! Oh my goodness, I couldn't believe it! Kate not only loved my article I wrote about my son, but she decided that she wanted to publish it in her online self-discovery magazine. This news filled me with so much happiness and confidence I felt like I could skip along the promenade where I live without ever needing to stop! Except reality kicked in and I realised that me and my knees, and palpitations, would not bode too well with the skipping lark, but it was a nice thought!

Kate Batten and I decided to keep in contact, not just regarding ideas from myself about writing for her magazine, but also to find out if the young girl needing treatment was doing ok. Within a month of knowing Kate, I was offered an amazing opportunity of being one of her online life coaches for her project, The Missing Piece Magazine.

I was absolutely thrilled at the new career path I was embarking upon and my mind became a whirlwind of creativity! How was I going to write my first article for the magazine? In what style, informal/formal, jovial or serious, focus on subject only or divert along different tangents? Yes, I have a mental health diagnosis, but that does not mean that I am devoid of any skills, abilities or ideas. I have an inquisitive mind and love to expand it in ways that only seek to challenge and inspire me.

My spell of good luck did not end there! Within the same month another unexpected opportunity presented itself to me. I was on my mobile searching 'how to become a TV extra'. I found an App called StarNow and proceeded to download it on my mobile. I set up my profile, added photos and built up the Credits section by including all the TV/Radio/Magazine/Newspaper interviews that I have done in the past with regards to my late-son's bone marrow donor appeal. I realised that I had quite a list! Within a few weeks of registering with the Casting Agency, I was receiving messages to invite me to auditions and to be a part of some worthwhile projects.

My first job was to play the role of a mum for a charity campaign video with regards to child abuse. It was a heart-breaking script but it was so important that the video got produced. There was such a vital message to convey to children and parents alike and I really appreciated being asked to be a part of this campaign.

After this job, I was asked if I would like to be in a comedy sketch for E4 Comedy Blaps. I jumped at the chance! I learned the script and had so much fun playing the role of a mum who catches her son online dating in his bedroom!

I met some lovely people who were passionate about the project they were involved in, who believed that they could achieve their goals - and they did! Around a month later, I received a message from two film producers who offered me the opportunity to meet them for an audition for their new short film. I was so excited! I kept thinking to myself...wow, what next?!

This new door of opportunity had opened up to me, and I made it happen! I made it happen because I believed in myself, I believed that I had the courage and the ability to fulfil my dreams.

In June 2017 I met the Producers and did my audition – for the role of a Police Officer – and they loved it! They offered me the role straight away! Wow, this was amazing! There I was auditioning for my first ever film role in front of two Producers and other aspiring actors, and because I was so passionate about re-inventing myself, and pushing the boundaries of what I thought I could achieve, I was now reaping the rewards of my persistence, fortitude and self-belief!

"All that we are is the result of what we have thought. The mind is everything. What we think we become." Buddha

With that thought in mind, here's the process of how we can train our minds to start believing in ourselves;

- When you write it you can start reading it.
- When you start reading it, you'll be able to start saying it.
- When you start saying it, you start hearing it.
- When you start hearing it, you start to believe it.
- When you believe it, things begin to change.
- When things begin to change, you will understand.
- When you understand, there will be clarity.

Only then will you truly start believing in yourself. From this new self-confidence that has grown like a flower in Spring time, you will realise your potential and become the person you have always aspired to be!

Don't just dream it.

Make it happen!

Still shot from the film 'Broken' 2017

Dream Big!

Feeling on top of the World

86th Floor of the Empire State Building 2017

Positive Affirmations

I am a good person

I have confidence in myself

I take care of my myself by dieting and exercise

I have the ability to accomplish anything

I am only human and I will make mistakes

I will never give up

I try my best at everything I do

I use my sense of humour to get me through my life journey

I surround myself with positive, compassionate people

I have control over my thoughts, feelings & emotions

I appreciate diversity and understand what equality means

I contribute my time to help others

I like to make a difference whenever I can

I love learning new things

I strive to best the best that I can be

I live my life my way

MAKE THOSE CHANGES TODAY!

CHAPTER 3
THE PRICE OF BRAVERY

Six Children, Mental Health, Money

WHAT IS THE PRICE OF BEING A PARENT? I am a busy mum of six children. Being a parent is no easy task. From the moment of conception, our lives are changed forever. It is a wonderful feeling to know that you have created a new life, a little person growing inside of you preparing itself for the big wide world. To think that human life is created from just 4 nitrogenous bases, A,C,G,T (adenosine/cytosine/guanine/thymine). How can these four letters create a living, breathing human being? With 206 bones; around 640 muscles; 11 systems i.e. (skeletal, immune, lymphatic); 32 teeth (adult); limbs; one brain, and a beating heart that keeps us alive! We are walking anatomical machines and we have been given the gift of life - that in itself is priceless. But how will we choose to spend this life? How many people will we encounter along our journey? Will becoming a parent be a part of your life path? Can money ever buy happiness? What will be 'our calling'?

Running a family home and managing my monthly budget has proved to be extremely stressful and difficult in the past. In order to overcome this issue I have had to be resourceful and also have needed to find the courage to ask for help, which is not easy for some people to do. There is a wealth of charitable organisations and benefit entitlements that are available to people if they meet the necessary criteria. These sources of potential income can be life-

42

saving when money becomes scarce and all feels lost.

Over the past few years my life has changed dramatically after getting divorced, and with that came repercussions. I ended up in a situation I never thought could happen...living alone without my precious children and having to rely on state benefits in order to put food on the table and a roof over my head. I have worked in Health & Social Care over the past few years and worked as a Domiciliary Care Worker, Support Worker and Housing Warden.

Whilst working in this sector, I witnessed incidents that I have only read about in the newspapers or seen on the news. I was horrified to work in an environment where I saw the older generation being shouted at, manhandled during personal care, and put to sleep in the afternoon so that the staff could have a rest.

During my time working in a care home I questioned members of staff as to the nature of their behaviour towards the residents, of which I put to them in a diplomatic and calm manner. The response was neither calm or diplomatic, and I was informed that if I didn't like the way they [the staff] worked, then I should leave as I obviously did not fit into the same mindset as the rest of the staff.

I can remember many occasions where I would 'double-up' with another member of staff to provide personal care to the residents, only to find that some residents had soiled themselves. I was horrified to find out that there was a limit on the number of pad changes per day, and so some residents were left in their dirty, soiled-ridden pads for hours. I could not understand why this was common practice at the care home, and neither could the elderly members that resided there. I asked the other members of staff why on earth are we to leave the residents in such a degrading and inhumane situation knowing what the repercussions would be for the elderly person left to sit in their own urine or faeces for another few hours? The lame excuse that was given to me was that 'the residents were only permitted to have 2 pad changes a day'. I could not believe what I was told.

How on earth can another human being leave a frail, weak, elderly person to remain in such despicable conditions? I proceeded to ask the staff members if they would treat they own mother, father, or grandparents in the same manner? Of course, the answer was 'no', and so I asked them why they think it's acceptable then to leave the residents in this way? Again, I was informed that if I didn't like the way the care home was run or how the staff worked, I should leave.

It became apparent that my line of questioning was becoming an irritation. Perhaps in the same vein as how the residents where feeling after being left to sit in soiled pads for hours on end! Over the course of a few weeks, I began to notice that members of staff were refraining from getting into conversation with me in the staff room. Also, whilst walking around the hallways of the care home, I was beginning to be ignored. During my coffee breaks I started to feel isolated and out-casted due to staff members showing hostility and ignorance towards me. I knew I had hit a nerve by asking many questions during my employment, and even though it resulted in my resignation, I was glad I had my say and spoke up to protect the residents.

The final insult was my final pay cheque. My punishment did not end at me resigning from the care home. What better way to hurt someone than hurting their wallet! Instead of my monthly pay that I was due, I was deducted half of my wages. After all the long shifts I worked; all the juggling of rotas between my kids and work; all the struggles to overcome my mental health by seeking employment; after speaking up on behalf of the all the residents - I was given just half of my wages. That says a lot about the care home I was working for. I only hope that working practices and attitudes will change within this industry and the frail, weak, elderly individuals whom are reliant on this service will get the proper 'duty of care' that they deserve and pay for.

Even though I worked full time, I was still struggling financially. The type of jobs I was doing took a toll on my mental and physical health and I had to resign from them all. This meant relying solely on benefits as a means of income.

I became depressed and stressed and didn't know who to turn to get help. I started searching online and realised that there are charities who offer a one-off grant to help you out if you are facing financial difficulty. I also contacted my local Citizen's Advice Bureau for more information. I didn't realise at that time that there were so many resources available, and also compassionate people who were willing to help me out in my time of need.

When times were very difficult I relied on food banks that are held at local churches where I live. I use to pop along and hand in my voucher and was looked after by the volunteers who run the scheme. They showed me compassion, understanding and love which is far more than my own family have shown or are currently showing me. Complete strangers at my local church running such a worthwhile service who treated me with the same dignity and respect that I showed them. This service proved invaluable to me over the past few years as I didn't know what I would have done for me and my children without it.

Whilst enduring such a difficult time, my one bed flat was my only sanctuary to the outside world, but this came at a price! The flat was an absolute nightmare. You wouldn't let your pets live in it, let alone yourself! It was absolutely freezing, even with the old wall heaters on. The bedroom had black mould all over the window and windowsill; one of the walls had water dripping down it with black mould and remained constantly cold; the front door had a gap under the door so a draught would always find its way into the living room/kitchen - and as far as the Landlady was concerned there was nothing wrong with the flat and it was habitable. Really? Seriously!? I became unwell whilst living in the flat and always suffered from 'flu-like' symptoms. Whenever my children stayed they felt the same and some occasionally were physically sick.

Due to the poor conditions in my bedroom, I slept

in my living room/kitchen, but this proved a difficult and stressful task when my children stayed with me. The sleeping arrangement ended up like this - one of my children slept on the sofa, 3 on the floor with lots of quilts and pillows, and me laying parallel to the front door. Yes, the front door, with my face up against the damp, draught-ridden gap in order to protect my children from the cold and the outside world.

One day I woke up and said, 'right, enough is enough', so I decided to contact an Environmental Health Officer to do an inspection, upon which he deemed the property unfit for myself or my children to remain in. This then gave me the impetus to contact my local community mental health team and my Support Worker from a local domestic abuse charity to intervene on my behalf and help me to find a more suitable property. It took over a year, but the wait was worth it. I was offered a lovely one bed flat, very spacious and full of natural light, with central heating! Yes! A brand new flat, big rooms, and full of warmth for me and my children when they stayed over.

When faced with such traumatic circumstances, my body and mind became so stressed and tired. I started getting generalised pain all over my body every day; extreme tiredness; 'brain-fog'; anxiety; insomnia and shortness of breath. I went to see my GP and I ended up doing a few blood tests. After a few weeks my GP told me I was developing the onset of Fibromyalgia. I had not heard much of this illness before and so started to read up about it. I couldn't allow all that was happening in my life at that time to destroy me, so I put together an action plan to get myself feeling better, both mentally and physically.

I use to go for walks along the beach; started eating a healthier diet; took time out occasionally from everything to sit in silence; and cut out toxic people from my life. Sometimes, in order to heal our souls, we all need to just forget everything for a while and just 'be in the moment'. Just to sit still, calm, quiet, and to listen to ourselves breathe and be aware of what our body is doing. Then you will find inner peace and tranquillity. Mindfulness has worked for me over the years and it is something I still practice today.

I have faced issues over the years that I never thought I would have to deal with. Like the animal and microbial kingdoms, us humans are built to evolve and adapt to constantly changing environments. It is this inherent attribute that allows you and me to find the courage and motivation to make the necessary changes to our daily lives to help improve the environment we are living in. If we never take that first step, as a baby does, then we will never learn how to walk down our chosen pathway.

Try not to allow money or anyone in your life control you, instead, you take control of your life and make the changes happen!

BUDGET BUDDY

Incomings   **Outgoings**

CHAPTER 4
IT'S ALL IN THE MIND

"Fear not the evil of others for they will never possess your inner strength"

My beloved son

SO, WHERE DO I START THIS STORY? Having to type the words about my son in a past tense is indescribable, painful and still unbelievable.

My beautiful son Jamie very sadly passed away in December 2010 after succumbing to Acute Myeloid Leukemia. My world was turned upside down and I didn't know how I was going to get through the next second, minute, hour or day. Life stood still and so did my mindset. I couldn't even think about the next day because all I wanted to do was turn the clock back to a time when life was good and my son was healthy. But the harsh reality of knowing that I couldn't do anything about the very sad passing of my son cut to the core. It defied the natural order of things. Part of me died with my beloved son. I was in a state of shock, despair, bewilderment and I couldn't foresee anything good happening or life changing for the better, how could I? But then I remembered how hard I fought to try to save Jamie's life and the strategy I put in place to try to achieve my ultimate goal.

I am the sort of person who has a growable mindset and I strive to achieve goals and turn negatives into positives, even when it seems there are none.

In 2005 when my son was diagnosed at Great Ormond Street Hospital with his rare illness, Fanconi Anemia, I was informed that it would take a long time to find a donor as my son not only had an extremely rare disease, but also a rare tissue type. Therefore, finding a compatible donor was going to prove a very challenging task for G.O.S.H. The Consultants informed me that they would look worldwide for a donor, but they would look to the UK and Malta first, as Jamie had Maltese heritage. After a few days it came to light that the island of Malta did not have a bone marrow donor registry or tissue type laboratory. If this facility had been in place, the potential to find a donor within a reasonable time span would have been reduced significantly.

On the way back home from Jamie's diagnosis in April 2005, I was quiet with my own thoughts and emotions running through my mind. I kept thinking to myself "what can I do to help?"; "how can I make enquiries about a potential donor registry?"; "how can I teach myself about my son's illness?".

From this moment on, even up until the present day, I am still campaigning to help save the lives of those in need and to try to make a difference....surely that's what being a human being is about? Not about material objects, not about just wanting to receive with no intention of ever giving back.

Surely, we are all put on the planet for a purpose, a reason for our existence, and it's only when we experience different circumstances, incidents, etc. that it may become apparent to us the answer(s) we are looking for. In 2005 after my son's diagnosis, I did one simple thing, I typed up an appeal letter for my local newspaper and emailed it to them. Within a few weeks Jamie's story was front page news and I was receiving calls from many local and national newspapers and magazines. Over the years that followed I had managed to gain worldwide exposure for Jamie's bone marrow donor appeal.

The media opportunities that arose were amazing and I met some very influential people who showed compassion and support. I was defiant that I was going to find a way to help save Jamie's life! Even though all the staff at Great Ormond Street Hospital were striving to find a donor and provided ongoing treatment as and when necessary. As Jamie's mum, I couldn't just sit back and wait for the phone to ring with news of a potential donor!

I am the type of person that doesn't give up when faced with adversity, instead I embrace the situation, consider my options, any restrictions, or opportunities to make changes etc. to achieve my goal. In 2006 Jamie's donor appeal had snowballed and even up until today I still keep Jamie's legacy alive. In 2008 two amazing things happened! One was the much-awaited telephone call from GOSH. They told me that they had found a Spanish donor who was a 95% match! My heart started racing, I was crying, my mind and body overwhelmed by this life saving phone call! My beloved Jamie was going to receive his lifeline, the one thing that stood between life and death. My heart was full of hope and excitement, but I put myself in Jamie's shoes, he was just a 10-year-old boy whose body was being pumped daily with medication or transfusions, and there we both were in our kitchen in July 2008, with the most amazing news we could have wished for!

It became apparent that 2008 was going to be a very tough year. But with the help and support of my Maltese friend who is a journalist for a popular Maltese newspaper, perhaps 2008 was going to become 'The Year of Change'.

Team work between myself and the Journalist finally paid dividends and Jamie's donor appeal gained interest and exposure in Brussels....yes finally, my beloved Jamie's appeal was discussed at the European Parliament, where it was agreed that Malta would receive EU funding and help in order to set up the island's first ever bone morrow donor registry/tissue-type laboratory. Wow! now news like that was unprecedented !! Just like the call from

GOSH!

In October 2008, Jamie received his bone marrow transplant and the weeks that followed were harrowing, not just for me to witness as Jamie's mum, but for Jamie to endure. The small yellow bag of stem cells that was administered via IV into my beloved son via his Hickman line, was either going to prove a success, or a tragic failure. Six long weeks later, me and my Jamie walked out of the main entrance of GOSH, got into our car and drove home, just in time for Christmas! This day was a miracle! It was the best gift me and Jamie could ever receive!

Very sadly, in December 2010, my beautiful Jamie passed away at home after 5 years of battling his illness. No words can describe the moment when you watch your own child take their last breath, to witness the pain their body is going through, and the sparkle dwindling from their eyes until the tragic moment when the room stands still and silent. To this very day I am still in shock and despair at losing my sweet son.

I am determined in my quest to help the island of Malta set up a donor registry or tissue type laboratory. Jamie's life will not be in vain and I will make his legacy live on to help save the lives of others, after all, that's what my son would have wanted. Jamie was the epitome of a sweet, kind, caring human being, and I take that strength and courage from him to be the best that I can be.

MINDSET

Our mind is a powerful tool enabling us to use our 5 unique senses to better understand the World around us. Who are we? What do we really want out of life? How can we make those changes? What if I have a fixed mindset?

What type of mindset do you think you have? Would you be prepared to change it to one that will open up a whole new life to you? The person that is shining within, with bundles of potential, but struggle to shine due to limitations in your life, albeit personal or business. Within the general population it is said that 40% of people have a fixed mindset versus 40% of people that possess a growth mindset vs 20% mixed.

Fixed Mindset

- You tend to give up easily on tasks
- You ignore criticism
- You blame others for you lack of success
- You assume effort is not necessary
- Your level of intelligence does not require expanding upon
- You allow setbacks to define you

Growth Mindset

- You embrace challenges
- You see setbacks as opportunities

- You take responsibility for your actions
- You want to stretch yourself to discover your true potential
- You are inspired by the success of others
- You see life as a journey

3 Types of Mental Contrasting

- What category do you feel you fall in to?
- What is holding you back?
- When can you implement change?
- How can you implement change?
- Who would support you?
- Who is holding you back?

INDULGING

- Optimistic
- Materialistic
- Top of the class
- Feels superior to others

DWELLING

- Pessimistic
- Struggles with obstacles
- Quits at the first hurdle
- Low self-worth

MENTAL CONTRASTING

- Loves a challenge!
- Self-belief
- Perseverance
- A 'can-do' attitude

Mindset: The Human Brain

The human brain is a very powerful muscle. It has the amazing ability to allow us to learn new things, to remember and have those 'déjà vu' moments, it allows us to use our emotional toolbox as and when needed, dependent on which situation(s) we are faced with.

Every time you and I learn something new, parts of our brain change and get bigger to compensate for the amount of new information. Inside the cortex of our brain there are approximately 100 billion nerve cells called neurons. These neurons act as an 'information highway' as they gather and transmit electrochemical signals.

The brain is hard-wired with connections, just like a computer. In the case of our brain however, the connections are made by neurons that link the sensory inputs and motor outputs with centres in the various lobes of the cerebral cortex. Memory is at the heart of all knowledge and understanding and there are many different methods that we can use in order for us to retain information and build upon our learning skills.

We all have our own way of learning and the tools we use could be any of the following: visual images, list writing, mnemonics, writing down thoughts and ideas, or by turning information into stories to make it easier for you to remember. Find the tools that you need to make the changes in your life that you want. What is right for one person is not necessarily right for another.

Never allow anyone to make you feel as if they 'own you', trying to control you or dictate your life'! Look deep within your heart and soul and believe in yourself! Always remember this, life cannot continue without the ability for growth!

MAKE UP YOUR MIND

What do you truly want?

CHAPTER 5
WHAT AM I WORTH?

What is self-esteem and what triggers it?

WHAT IS SELF-ESTEEM? Well, it is about how you believe in yourself and the confidence you possess with regards to your own abilities and values. How do you feel about yourself and your capabilities? Do you feel like a failure? That you're an underachiever? That people are always laughing at you and not with you? No matter what level your self-esteem is at, it can have a pretty huge effect on your life, from your relationships with loved ones, to co-workers, family and friends.

Have you ever wondered why you have such low self-esteem? What is happening in your life right now to make you feel that way? Or what has prevailed in your past? Some of the feelings and emotions you are going through could be related to many reasons. Do you recognise, or can you relate to any of these?

- Loneliness
- bullied – as a child, teenager or adult
- underachieved at school/college
- neglect or abuse – physical or mental
- being unemployed
- being used as a 'scapegoat'
- being told you are fat, ugly or stupid?
- feeling unloved and that you don't deserve to be

loved or happy?

Sometimes it can be hard to identify the causes of your low self-esteem. Perhaps you've never really thought about it, or maybe it's difficult to determine when it first started. Whether or not you know exactly what's causing it, there are steps you can take to build your confidence and improve the way you feel about yourself.

10 steps for improving your self-esteem

1. Positive attitude

If like me, you have told yourself in the past that you are no good, over time you might just start believing it, even though you know it's not true! Don't let the negativity of others define who you are, or who you want to be!

2. Don't compare yourself to others

In the past I have tried to compare myself to others in my social network and this have proved to be very debilitating. We are all great at our own things, albeit work, hobbies, bringing up children etc, so try not to compare yourself to others, for we all have our own set of strengths and weaknesses.

3. Movement and exercise

Exercise is a great way of coping with day-to-day stress and helping us have some time out from the issues we have on our minds. I enjoy walking and listening to music to help me come to terms with my daily stresses. Sometimes I listen to Hip Hop, Classical or Dance music, and other times I may listen to Tibetan meditation. This helps me to incite ideas and positivity!

4. Perfection is...

What I have come to realise is that no one is perfect! Striving for perfection is exhausting! Just try and be the best that you can be, without any unnecessary or unachievable goals/targets. This will only put added stress on you otherwise.

5. We all make mistakes!

Let's be honest, if we didn't make mistakes we wouldn't be human! Just try and learn from mistakes you've made and find ways to manage problems by choosing a different mindset. Sometimes it's the most simple approach to something that we don't look for, opting for overthinking, then making a mistake!

6. Focus on the things you can change

Energy is very time consuming on your body and mind. So try not to waste too much energy on situations that are out of your control, instead, focusing your energy on those that are.

7. Do things you enjoy

Do things in your life that make you happy! Perhaps a relaxing bath with candles; a walk in the park; painting, or joining a local singing group? It doesn't matter what it is, so long as it keeps you happy. And remember, your happiness is detrimental to your well-being, so put aside any negativity from others!

8. Feel a sense of achievement

Why not celebrate the achievements you have made in your life, no matter how big or small! It could be finally managing to open your post; meeting up with friends; speaking up for yourself; cooking dinner or even managing to leave your home for the first time in ages! Pat yourself on the back, as only you know how difficult that task can be for you.

9. Be helpful and considerate

Be mindful of those that are close to you and help to support them as much as they support you. This two-way relationship can work wonders for you by boosting your sense of self-worth, self-love, and self-confidence.

10. Surround yourself with like-minded people

In order to remain positive, cheerful and confident about yourself, socialise with people who share a similar mindset to you. In my own experience, socialising with certain family members and co-workers only brought me down and made me depressed due to their toxic, self-centred, hostile personalities. So now I choose to have a small network of friends that share the same way of thinking as me, and who only seek to project love, support, positivity and laughter.

Who or what is affecting your self-esteem?

In my own personal life, my self-esteem was shattered after enduring years of domestic abuse in my marriage. I was made to feel worthless; stupid; insecure; anxious; and that I was always to blame. Abusive individuals are insecure, weak and lack self-confidence, hence why they treat loved ones or people they know with such hostility and ridicule. Always remember that you are beautiful, on the inside and out, and those that tell you otherwise have core issues about themselves that they do not have the courage to face, so instead impart their negative attitude on to you. It's their way of lying to themselves that they can be like you, except deep down within their soul, they know that they don't possess the qualities that you do.

Since walking away from my marriage and getting divorced, my family and some of my extended family have disowned me and have shown nothing but hostility, which absolutely beggar's belief. So how does this all make me feel? Well, at the beginning of this nightmare, I started to think that I had done the wrong thing by leaving my husband and that perhaps the abuse was all in my mind? I started to doubt myself as a mother, daughter, sister, auntie and also as a human being.

Then as the months and years passed, and abuse was thrown my way by my family, I came to realise that it's far easier to make me a scapegoat than to help and support me at a time when I need them the most. After all, what have my family got to gain by helping me to fight my corner and support me?

My family's actions, or lack of, have made me feel like the black-sheep of the family; that I am incapable of being a good mother and person; that I am mentally ill; that I don't deserve my beloved children; that I am deranged. It took many years of heartache and tears to come to the conclusion that I will NOT be bullied or harassed by anyone, and that I am a good person.

The late-Edmond Locard (1877-1966) Professor of Forensic Medicine at University of Lyons in France, stated that 'every contact leaves a trace'. The idea behind Locard's thinking was that whenever someone interacts with something 'they leave a trace of themselves and at the same time pick up something from the interaction'. This statement is quite profound and relevant with regards to the incidents and circumstances I have witnessed or been involved in over my lifetime so far. I am of the opinion that 'Locard's Principle' is relevant to any and every aspect of our life on earth.

Since 2014, I have gradually become a confident, strong-willed, determined woman and there is no way I am backing down now! Yes, I have lost everything over the years, but it's how we choose to deal with such traumatic circumstances that dictates how we come to terms with a new chapter in our lives. During the difficult times, my only source of comfort was when I saw my children, and also the fact that I have in my possession my late-son's Urn and personal effects. I will not be silenced, I will not be manipulated, I will not be controlled - I will be me!

How many of these symptoms can you relate to?

Fearful

Sexual dysfunction

Hypersensitivity

Isolation

Self-sabotaging

Depression

Unreasonable expectations

Workaholic

Boundary issues

Self-defeating behaviour

Lack of self-confidence

Hypervigilance

OCD

Psychology of the mind

Self-esteem is non-discriminate - it can affect any gender, age, ethnicity, religion or race. We as humans have the ability to experience many emotions, and it's the philosophy we choose to use that allows us to be unique. One quote that I thought of in 2017 and have decided to include in this book is this - 'Do not let the behaviour of others ever determine who you are, but let it give you the strength to fulfil your dreams!'

The late-Dr Nathaniel Branden was a Canadian–American psychotherapist and writer who was known for his work in the 'psychology of self-esteem' and focused on developing his own psychological theories and modes of therapy. One quote of Dr Branden's that I like is, "The first step toward change is awareness. The second step is acceptance". This rings true with my own life and I am sure many of you reading this. If we can open-up our minds and be mentally and physically aware of our own self, then this can educate us onto a higher level, which in turn will naturally follow to the path of acceptance.

The mind is a very powerful organ which stores infinite information and is constantly updating like my iMac that I typed this book on. But remember, my iMac and our brains are machines, and we can control machines. An analogy that I would like to use is this - just like my computer, I back up files in my mind and put some in the recycle bin, and some in a temporary folder, should I need to recall some information in the future. But I dictate what script I want to read in my head. To lose control of my inner thoughts would be detrimental to me in so many ways, so I endorse a positive, upbeat personality to help guide me to a better life.

MY POSITIVE TRAITS

MY NEGATIVE TRAITS

CHAPTER 6
GRATITUDE

What Should We Be Grateful For?

THIS IS QUITE A POWERFUL QUESTION to ask with a multitude of possible answers. We can all be grateful for many things in this life, things which are all relevant to who we are and what we hope to achieve. Should we be grateful for the air we breathe? The easy access to water? The roof over our head? Perhaps the car we drive or the latest phone we possess?

In the English Dictionary, the word 'Gratitude' means... the quality of being thankful; readiness to show appreciation for and to return kindness.

I asked my children what they are grateful for in their lives and the five of them responded with these answers:

1. Wifi
2. Xbox One
3. Waterpolo
4. Gift of Life
5. My Girlfriend & Marvel Movies!

I thought their answers were endearing, and I also realised that in a way they are non-discriminate, i.e. how are the answers of my four children any different from that of an adult? What about if you have everything? How many celebrities are truly happy with the possessions they own and the numbers in their bank account? How must it feel to wake up every morning knowing that money is no object and you could spend your day purchasing goods, services etc. for material objects that perhaps you don't even need or want? So, what does a person hope for when they have everything? Surely the only thing we can ever have enough of is breathing?

This profound statement made me think deeply about us as human beings and what our core basic needs are, of which have never changed over the passage of time. It's only due to the technological advances over the past 20 years that has changed the dynamics of someone's personality, home, relationship, hopes and dreams.

With the advent of social media, different advertising platforms across road and railway systems, pop-up ads on devices, and the 'sexual innuendos' within TV commercials, this has, and is, all having a negative impact on us humans and distorting our minds and values as to what is really important in our daily lives. But obviously that is my opinion and I do not expect everyone to agree.

I recently watched a very interesting and insightful documentary on TV called Wild China. The episode I watched was about the indigenous people of Tibet and how they live off the land and lead a very happy life. Tibet, which is in South West China, has a vast plateau which is home to a culture of people whom are shaped by Buddhism.

The Tibetan Plateau is one of the largest land-based wilderness areas left in the world. It is a global eco-region and is referred to by many as the "Roof of the World". At its peak the Tibetan Plateau connects landscapes from

Europe, Asia and the Middle East. Tibet is blessed with mountains and glaciers which provide vital life support for HALF the planet! The wildlife is abundant with jewel-coloured birds, elephants, yaks, antelopes and snow leopards.

The indigenous tribes in Tibet are testament to what it is to be human. To appreciate the gift of life itself. To give thanks for the food, water, shelter and love that is uniquely abundant and precious between the human and mammal kingdoms.

So why are so many people depressed and lonely even though they possess such bountiful riches? Why do human beings feel this way when they have acquired material objects, wealth and love, and yet many have still not found inner happiness and peace?

MY FOUR SEASONS OF LIFE

The blossoming of flowers

The sound of bird song

The smell of Daffodils

The brighter days

* * * * * *

The sun on your face

The sandcastles made with my kids

The abundance of smiles

The romantic walks along the beach

* * * * * *

The winds of change

The spectrum of colours

The crunch of the leaves

The cool breeze in the air

* * * * * *

The beauty of a blanket of snow

The mesmerising light of a candle

The new beginnings

The new you!

When I think of the word 'gratitude' I think of my beloved children, for without them I am nothing, but with them I am everything. There are many things we can be grateful for in this world, but the most important thing is the gift of life! I believe that each and every one of us has been put on this mortal earth for a reason – and when we have achieved our purpose, our reason for being, then it will be our time to move on to the next life.

The Maltese Cross in memory of Jamie

As I have mentioned, I very sadly lost my beloved 12 year old son to acute myeloid leukemia in December 2010. After years battling his illness and years of medical procedures, my beloved son finally succumbed to his illness. I only wish that I could turn back time, like so many other parents in my shoes, and have just one more day with him - to see his face again, his smile, the 'love of life' in his eyes, playing computer games with him and just hearing him call me 'mum'. I would give up everything right now to have that moment again.

But the very sad reality is that that 'moment' can never happen. So how do parents in my shoes come to terms with this gut-wrenching, traumatic, living nightmare? The only way I know how to cope with such a huge void in my life is to concentrate on the positives, whatever they may be. I think of my beautiful children and how they fill me with joy and happiness. I think of how fate blessed me with the gift of my beloved son, if only for 12 years.

Due to the nature of my son's illness, he could have passed away at any time after he was diagnosed in 2005. So, I have thought deeply about the fact that me and my beloved son were blessed with, not only the 12 years we had together, but those 5 years between 2005 to 2010 that he fought his illness until he finally left this mortal earth.

During the years 2005 to 2010, my beloved Jamie and I developed a bond that would take most parents a life-time. We spent so much time together and got to know each other so well as mother and son that we were inseparable. I gave him strength and love on days when he felt all was lost, and equally, my beloved Jamie reciprocated that.

The human race is dependent on the same core basic needs, as created by the late-Abraham Maslow in his

'Hierarchy of Needs' (1943). It is these core basic needs that we depend and rely on every day which inherently makes us human.

Wealth and possessions are all a bonus of which we should all be grateful for. But how many people in this world are facing poverty / abuse / homelessness, or dealing with a serious health issue, especially cancer, and are unable to afford necessary medication? How can it be fair for so many people to be suffering in silence without any emotional or financial support to help alleviate the harsh dilemmas they are faced with on a daily basis?

When the going gets tough – act on it! Don't bury your head in the sand and wait for the difficulties of life to pass you by. Don't depend on others to achieve the results you are looking for. Embrace your fears head-on, with an open mind and heart and seek to find the solution(s) to your problems. They may not come easy or for free – but just know this, they will come to you! The Universe will expand your mind, in the same way that it expands itself. Ask the Universe for help in your time of need and it shall deliver. Perhaps not when and how you expected, but it will dive deep down into your very soul and show you how to fix what has been broken. And if it ain't broke – yep, I hear ya! - don't fix it!!

JAMIE'S BONE MARROW DONOR APPEAL

2005-2016

Below is an email that I sent to a local paper in order to keep my son's legacy alive and to be able to turn a massive negative into something positive – to help save the lives of other people.

Email to local newspaper in 2016 -

Hello, my name is Donna Pace and I live in Weymouth. I lost one of my children to Acute Myeloid Leukemia 5 years ago after undergoing a bone marrow transplant at Great Ormond Street Hospital. Since 2005 I have been tirelessly campaigning for members of the public to consider donating blood and becoming a potential bone marrow donor by appealing to local, national and international press and media.

In May 2008 I asked the Maltese Government why they do not have a donor database and if this will ever be considered as a viable option? I took my appeal to the European Parliament in May 2008, where it was decided that the island of Malta would get help in setting up a donor registry in the future.

Since this time, I have met with two Directors from Anthony Nolan in London, and I also flew over to Malta to meet with the Prime Minister's Private Secretary in Dec 2013 to get an update regarding the registry, and to also explain, on a personal level, why I felt that my late-son's story would help the Maltese Government to understand the human element in such a project, in order to persuade the Private Secretary to consider such a project. With that in mind, there is also the realization that logistically, it would take many years to complete.

I have been working tirelessly to try to bring the two entities together - Anthony Nolan and the Maltese Government. It doesn't appear that much progress has been made so I am looking to set up another meeting with Maltese Government officials to inject some energy and passion behind a very worthwhile cause.

I would very much appreciate it if you could help me with my appeal by publishing this story and adding some weight behind a project of which I know my late-son would be very proud of me for achieving. This appeal is not just about my late-son, it's about turning a negative situation into a positive one by way of continuing my late-son's legacy to help save the lives of others across the World.

I thank you for your time in reading this email. I look forward to hearing from you.

With kind regards

Miss Donna Pace

BONE MARROW DONOR APPEAL –

PRESS & MEDIA CAMPAIGN 2005-2016

2016 Local Newspaper story

2015   Wessex FM interview in aid of Anthony Nolan Charity

2013 Meeting with Maltese Prime Minister's Private Secretary

2013 Meeting with Anthony Nolan Directors with regards to setting up a donor registry

2009 BBC Radio 5 Live - Victoria Derbyshire

2009 BBC News Interview - Ayshea Buksh & Evening Standard

2008 Take A Break Magazine

2008 News of The World & Daily Mail

2008 Jamie's Bone Marrow Donor Appeal discussed at the European Parliament in Brussels. Victor Vella – Maltese Journalist wrote Jamie's story and was awarded 'Journalist of the Year' in Malta.

2008 Telephone interview with CNN London

2008 ITV This Morning Show - Eamonn Holmes and Ruth Langsford

2008 Live on CH4 - Jon Snow

2007 Women's Own Magazine

2007 Malta – TV interview – debate show

2007 Malta – live radio interview

2007 BBC Radio Solent – live interview

2007 ITV late night debate show – London Talking with Connie Huq, Vanessa Feltz and Nick Ferrari

2007 Sky News interview

2006 ITV This Morning Show with Philip Schofield and Fern Britton

2006 I produced and printed at home 400 donor appeal leaflets of which I took up to London to pass on to the Chairman of the Maltese Culture Movement Club

2006 Charity Walk with Royal Bank of Scotland in London in aid of Jamie's appeal and Anthony Nolan Charity

2005 Local newspapers covering Jamie's story

How do I end this chapter knowing that the ending fills me with dread and such a heavy heart? I wanted to share my story about my beautiful Jamie because I need to feel like he is still with me, if only in spirit. My Jamie would have been 22 years old this year. For me, so many memories, hugs, kisses, wishes, dreams all lost, never to be created again. What I do have, however, are all the fond memories of me and Jamie since the moment I brought him into this world, and equally, when he very tragically left it.

I will continue with my plan to work with the Maltese Government to set up a tissue-type laboratory or bone marrow donor register. My late-son's legacy will live on forever and help to re-start the lives of those in need.

R.I.P Jamie. XXXX

WHAT I AM GRATETFUL FOR?

CHAPTER 7
NEW YORK CITY BABY!

IT WAS 05.30AM ON A VERY COLD wintery morning on 5th January 2017. I was getting into a taxi with my new suitcase and a huge smile on my face! I was full of excitement, optimism and hope. After 45 years on this planet, it was now time for me to embark on an amazing journey. On the way to London Heathrow airport so many ideas and thoughts raced through my mind. How did such a 'once-in-a-lifetime' opportunity be given to me? It was a dream-come true. To know that I was going to one of the biggest cities in the world, on my 45th Birthday – how awesome is that?!

When I arrived at Heathrow airport around 10.30am, the first thing I saw was the huge terminal where I needed to check-in, and the illuminated signs for 'Virgin Atlantic/Delta' airlines. I had to pinch myself as I couldn't quite believe that I was actually there, like literally!! After all the trials and tribulations in my life so far, there I was, walking into the entrance of Terminal 3 to check-in for my American adventure!

Many emotions were running through my mind – quicker than Usain Bolt can do 100 metres, (not including the last race of his career!). Sorry Mr Bolt, I am a huge fan of yours, honest! Anyway, where was I? Oh yeah, at Terminal 3. I was checked-in and sitting alone in the departure lounge. Not at any point since I left home early that morning had I felt lonely, scared or shy. I felt liberated and alive! In the departure lounge I was 'people watching', seeing how members of the public interacted with one another and listened to their conversations about their impending trip to New York City.

I gripped my seat with both hands whilst listening to the roar of the airplane engines engaging, preparing the plane for 'full-thrust' mode, whilst taxing onto the runway. My children's faces were popping up in my head and I was going through each image like a reel of old film negatives, skipping from picture to picture. Each image filling my heart with warmth, love, and a new 'sense of self'. The plane started its ascent into the big blue sky, at which point I clutched tightly the butterfly necklace around my neck which is embedded with my beloved late-son's fingerprint. I closed my eyes, held the silver butterfly necklace close to my chest, and said quietly to myself, 'thank you Jamie son, thank you for making my dream come true'.

At 10.30pm CET, I landed at JFK airport. I disembarked from the plane and walked towards the Customs Terminal. I was greeted by a polite and friendly Customs Officer who checked my passport and asked the necessary security questions. I'll never forget that Customs Officer – he wished me a 'Happy Birthday' and also said that I was a brave woman to take a holiday to NYC alone! This comment filled me with laughter, confidence and excitement all in one go!

I boarded my shuttle bus with lots of other tourists and we were all in awe at the sights and sounds of New

York City. The driver was taking each of us to our destinations, and it just so happened that I was the first tourist to be dropped off at my chosen hotel – the Waldorf Astoria, 301 Park Avenue, baby!! I picked up my suitcase and pulled it along behind me like a little dog, talking to it, giggling and laughing. It was absolutely freezing whilst walking towards the entrance of the hotel, but I didn't care. I would have braved a storm!

The lights shone through the revolving doors of the hotel and all I could see was marble flooring, huge chandeliers and lots of people, from all walks of life. Woohoo! Here I am New York City! I was a bit nervous walking through the Lobby towards the Reservations Desk – I stood and looked around me at the beautiful interior of one of the World's most amazing hotels. I was welcomed by a lovely lady who was astute enough to realise that it was my birthday. She then proceeded to wish me a 'Happy Birthday' and gave me complimentary drinks vouchers. 'Well this is nice', I thought! I could not have asked for a better introduction to American soil than that! I walked around the Lobby to locate one of the many lifts within the hotel. My room was on the 22nd Floor. I got into the lift and pressed number 22. Whoosshh! The wind from the lift shaft expelled through the door as I propelled from the 1st to the 22nd floor!

My feet walked on the beautiful, lush carpet along the opulent hallway towards my room. When I walked in I thought I was in the wrong room, but it turned out I wasn't. The Waldorf Astoria had very generously upgraded me! Where do the surprises end?! I rushed into my room, embracing every aspect of it – opening doors, cupboards, sitting at the desk, on the sofas, checking out the bathroom, eventually ending up sitting on the huge windowsill. I pulled back the massive cream curtains to reveal one of my all-time favourite buildings in the World – the Chrysler building! I sat on the windowsill staring down at the roads beneath me whilst listening to the sounds of NYC at night. I was speechless (well, not that I had anyone to share this experience with anyway!). But I didn't need or want anyone to be with me – just me. A trip to help me find out who I am and what I am made of.

The three nights and three days I spent in the Big Apple did not disappoint me. My holiday exceeded my expectations of what I thought it would be like to venture in and around Manhattan. I spent my time wisely and crammed in lots of sightseeing with lots of Starbucks coffees! I walked so much and yet it didn't bother me. Once I left my hotel every day and exited from the revolving door, I was zapped up into NYC life! Within 72 hours I had managed to visit the following attractions:

- Empire State Building
- Rockefeller Center
- Statue of Liberty
- Ellis Island
- Times Square
- Grand Central Station
- Bloomingdale's (for coffee, cake and retail therapy!) I bought a big bottle of Coco Mademoiselle (still have over ¾ left to this day!)
- SAKS on 5th
- One World Trade Center
- Central Park & Central Park Zoo
- Late Night Tour Bus (round trip) around Manhattan & Brooklyn

Having fun in Times Square!

The one and only cool Lady, the Statue of Liberty!

Whilst sitting in Bloomingdale's eating my coconut and raspberry cake whilst washing it down with a regular latte, I noticed through the huge window a homeless man sitting in a wheelchair covered in thick winter clothes with a blanket over his legs. I sat and watched how members of the public walking around the street, and in and out of the stores, were just walking past this gentleman as if he did not exist. I could not bear to sit in the warmth of the café knowing that there was another human being opposite the street, sitting in the snowy, freezing conditions, with no one saying 'hello'. So, I put down my food and drink and left. I walked around the street looking for a McDonalds, of which I found very quickly! I ordered a large Big Mac Meal and Coffee.

I wasn't sure if I was doing the right thing but I carried on with my plan. I crossed the huge road and started to walk towards the homeless man. First of all, I introduced myself and explained that I was across the road when I noticed him. The gentleman was ever so polite and engaging and told me his name was Eddie. 'Hi Eddie', I said, 'it's a pleasure to meet you. I hope you don't mind but I have bought you a hot meal and drink'. Eddie did not know what to say, he looked shocked – not just by my generosity, by I think also by the fact that someone had stopped to talk to him.

There was such a beautiful sense of humanity and warmth about Eddie that compelled me to stay and chat with him. I remember the conversation as if it were yesterday. I explained to Eddie that I was on holiday in NYC from the UK and that I didn't think it was right that we all share this planet, and yet some people are faced with such hardships. I asked Eddie if I could give him a hug, from one human being to another, and he said 'yes'. I hugged Eddie as tightly as I could to let him know that he is not alone and that there are people in this world that care about him. It was an emotional experience, a see-saw of emotions, knowing that I was able to spend time with him, and yet, it could only be for a short while. Who would talk, hug, feed, comfort Eddie when I left NYC? I am sure that many people have stopped to talk to Eddie, if only for 5 mins. Well, that's what I hope anyway. None of us know how or why people end up in the situations they do, and therefore, we should never judge, for we do not know their life or what they have experienced.

After returning back to the UK from my awesome trip, I was filled with a new sense of self-belief. I felt liberated! A brand-new woman! A brand new me! Yay! I was not prepared to let anyone make me feel any differently! It had taken a huge leap of faith in myself to travel to NYC alone, but I did it – even to the surprise of my mental health team that continue to support me.

If you have had to face your fears alone, then just imagine what you can achieve with supportive, like-minded, positive people by your side! Life is for living to its fullest – so go on, what are you waiting for? Yes you, reading my book right now! Your life will not change unless you put on your 'brave hat' and venture off into the unknown. Never look at mistakes as failures, look at them as experience. Good luck x

DESTINATIONS I HAVE BEEN TO

DESTINATIONS ON MY BUCKET LIST

CHAPTER 8
LOVE & LAUGHTER

MY ALARM GOES OFF AT 9AM, it's sunday, so i don't bother getting up. I decide to stay in bed, it's my weekend off without my kids, it's raining outside and my joints are stiff, so i'm going nowhere fast! I always like to phone my kids when they're not with me, so i lean over my bed, with much discomfort and oohhing and aarrrgging, and pick up my mobile off my bedroom floor, with a newly acquired crack on the screen. My fingers are like sausages from water retention…it's not pretty being in your 40's! I click contacts on my mobile and phone my dentist instead of my son. With another click on my phone, i get it right, and i'm welcomed with a "hello mum, how are you"? This makes my day, and i continue to chat to my son tommy before i realise he is more hungover than martin sheen! Tommy's words are slurred, he's giggling more than a 2 month old baby whose parents are playing 'peekaboo', yet there is a sense of embarrassment in his voice. Why the embarrassment i thought? What's wrong with tommy? What happened to him last night whilst he was 'out on the lash?

Whilst I am thinking and dwelling on Tommy's demeanour, I can hear Tommy on the other end of the phone rambling away about something, but I couldn't make out what? What was this news or gossip that my son wanted to share with me? 'Hey Tommy', I said, 'you still sound hungover son, and I've never heard you laugh so much! Share the gossip with me son, I could do with a laugh!'

'Ok mum, haha, sorry, I can't contain myself! This will make you laugh, but maybe also hate me? I got absolutely battered last night'! Yeah, I can hear it in your voice son, you sound very relaxed, you sound like you're struggling to put two words together! Why would I hate you son? What an earth did you do last night? Oh god, don't tell me you got into a fight? You didn't get into a fight last night did you son?!

Tommy laughs at the end of the phone and tries to compose himself before he answers my questions. 'Oh no mum, definitely not, I'm a lover not a fighter! What I've done is far worse than that!' I shriek in despair…WHAT?!! Oh no son, what have you done?! My heart started racing, my mind became a minefield of emotions, so I walked over to my sofa, sitting gently in anticipation of what I was about to hear. I can remember the last time I felt like this, it was the 20th January 2017, the day Trump was inaugurated!

OK Tommy, you know I love you no matter what, I'm your Mum, here to protect and serve! Tommy's voice becomes a bit subdued and the giggling seems to be easing off. Tommy hesitates before he discloses the much awaited gossip that I am desperate to hear.

'Please don't judge me Mum, like I said, I got absolutely battered last night, and don't remember a thing! Erm, when I got home last night, I obviously panicked and have no idea why, and I eh, took a crap in the bloody washing machine! I am so disappointed with myself, I am such a twat! I feel horrible, how do I even apologise for that'?! Are you kidding son? You took a crap in the machine?!

Tommy replied with a combination of laughter and humiliation in his voice. 'I don't remember doing so, but it would appear so! I know, I'm an idiot'! You're not an idiot son, far from it! You're a beautiful human being and I'm proud to say that you're my son. 'Washing machines live longer with crap-on!' - I sung this to Tommy in the style of the TV advert for Calgon! 'You know what makes it worse', Tommy said. 'I didn't do it for the banter, at least then it would've been a practical joke! I literally was just in the mindset that I am in the bathroom'.

Yeah right son I said, that old chestnut! Hey Tommy, you fancy coming round for dinner this week? I'd love to see how you managed to squat down and contort your body to fit your bottom in the machine?!

I couldn't get my breath for laughing too much in disbelief at what Tommy had told me!

'Yeah sure mum, I'd love to pop round for dinner, what day? By the way, what are the dimensions of your washing machine'!? Excuse me, what son? What are the dimensions? Why? You're not thinking of taking a crap in my machine are you? Most people generally do that on my doorstep! 'Erm, no mum, I won't be defecating in your machine, that's quite a unique art form, more of a spur of the moment thing'!

I didn't realise Tommy had such a great sense of humour and sense of fun! Not in the 21 years since giving birth to Tommy had I ever realised what an honest, funny, down-to-earth young man he has evolved into. Forgetting the fact that he took a dump in his dad's washing machine, and not even had the decency to fill the machine draw with a dash of bleach and put it on a 90 degree quick wash! Perhaps Tommy will never become a Washing Machine Engineer, but one thing is for sure, being a qualified Gym Instructor/Swimming Teacher has definitely paid dividends when it came to improvisation!

* * * * * *

What is Love?

When you stop and think about this question, we could all put together an infinite array of answers, for love is a unique emotion that has great meaning to each and every one of us. When we are born we are innocent, naïve and non-conformist. We have no knowledge of what is to come of our lives or how we are going to grow and develop. From the moment we are born we are conditioned – conditioned by the outside world from everyone that we will come into contact with.

An analogy that I like to use is this – imagine a piece of clay on its journey to become an object – perhaps a vase or a plate. An individual has an idea in their mind of what they want and how to make that happen. The process will start with the idea, then tangibly working with the materials necessary to create the end product. Except, in order to achieve their goal, there will be a process of working with the clay to manipulate, control and support it whilst endeavouring to reach the required goal.

Once the vase or plate etc. has been made, what home will it go to? Will it be put on show in the home or tucked away in a cupboard? Will this item be loved, cherished, or looked after? Will it prove to be of use only on occasions? This resonates with the creation of life itself and perhaps how some people envisage how they are going to adjust and cope with another person in their life? Will their nurture and love their 'vase' or will they choose to admire the 'vase' intermittently when their needs dictate?

Can anyone truly love another person unconditionally? What if some people spent their childhood, adolescence or adult life being unloved, ostracized or abused? How would these feelings and emotions affect the way they treat their own children, or the ones they love? Will that inherent sense of nurturing be lost and devoid within them or would they be able to delete the demons from their past and treat their child in the same manner as they had once hoped to be treated?

The expression of love starts the moment a baby is born. The overwhelming feeling a mother and father experience when they see their baby for the first time is one that will last with them forever. The creation of life is a miracle – one that should never be taken for granted, for we all come into this world with innocence and a thirst – a thirst for food, a thirst for knowledge, and a thirst to be loved.

What drives us to need to be loved?

The foundation of being happy as a human being is the need to be loved. We are happy when we are loved and we love to be happy. The desire to be loved results from the profound interdependence that we all share with one another.

It doesn't matter how wealthy or intelligent any person may be, the physiological effects of living a life being unloved could prove fatal. Every living creature on planet Earth, albeit the human, animal or microbial kingdoms, can only thrive and survive by the art of communication. Without communicating with one another, we all begin to feel isolated, lonely and depressed. These feelings can have detrimental effects on our emotional and physical self.

Humans, animals, and the microbial kingdoms all have their own unique way of communication with one another:

HUMAN

Speech / Braille / Sign Language / Body Language /

Auditory

ANIMAL

Visual / Auditory / Tactile / Chemical

(Whales sing, Wolves howl, Birds tweet & chirp)

MICROBIAL

Chemical through quorum sensing. This enables

bacteria to co-ordinate their behaviour.

The Law of Nature

'Interdependence is a fundamental law of nature. Even tiny insects survive by co-operating with each other. Our own survival is so dependent on the help of others that a need for love lies at the very core of our existence. This is why we need to cultivate a genuine sense of responsibility and a sincere concern for the welfare of others'. His Holiness the Dalai Lama.

The Law of Nature is determined by the mutual co-operation between all living organisms which is based on an innate recognition of one's interconnectedness. We can only thrive and proliferate through being loved and communicating with other people. This same rule applies to the animal and microbial kingdoms.

How can we make other people happy?

The answer(s) to this question is relevant to who we are, based on our own personal beliefs or opinions. What is the one thing today that has made you smile? Made you feel like your heart is light and devoid of worries, if only for a few minutes? What connection have you made today, this week or month with a new human being, an interaction which has given you a sense of hope or fulfilment?

I would like to think that I am a happy-go-lucky type of soul and I am not materialistic. I believe that simple pleasures in life can make us happy; the sound of bird song; the feeling of wind in your hair; the smile on your child's face when you collect them from school; devoting your time to care for individuals who are frail or unwell; perhaps winning a football bet; relaxing in a bath with candles? The list is endless and only relevant to who we are and what our definition of being happy is.

THE PHYSIOLOGICAL IMPACT OF STRESS

ON THE BODY

Mind: Worrying. Impaired judgment. Nightmares. Indecisiveness. Negative thoughts. Hasty decisions. Fearful.

Behaviour: Accident prone. Loss of appetite. Substance abuse. Insomnia. Loss of libido. Restlessness. Erratic.

Emotions: Lack of confidence. Irritable. Depression. Apathy. Alienation. Apprehensive. Low self-esteem. Hypersensitivity.

Body: Headaches. Frequent infections. Joint & muscular pain. Fatigue. Skin conditions. Breathlessness. Palpitations.

The Correlation between Mental Health and the deprivation of Love

I have no qualms about speaking about my mental health and the fact that I have Post Traumatic Stress Disorder. Coming to terms with this diagnosis and finding ways to deal with my symptoms is an on-going battle, but one I have to accept and live with. I was diagnosed with PTSD a few years ago due to the very tragic passing of one of my children and the years of domestic abuse I endured throughout my marriage.

It is astounding to think that the traumas I have witnessed and been exposed to are in the same vein as; 'combat stress reaction', 'shell shock', and 'war neurosis, of which was initially attributed to soldiers fighting in WWI, WWII and during the Vietnam War. Trauma and shock can have devastating effects on our physical and mental health of which can remain with us to our dying day.

Very sadly, no matter what media campaigns are being run across all social platforms, TV, radio etc. There is, and will always be, a stigma attached to individuals who suffer from mental health. A mindset which has been planted like a seed many years ago and allowed to grow and blossom into a 'taboo subject'.

Every individual has their own definition or personal opinion of what 'mental health' means, albeit whether this is right or wrong? It is a very sad fact that those individuals that possess or express judgmental, ignorant, or disparaging remarks are more often than not those that are closest to you.

From my own personal experience, any negativity surrounding my mental health has emanated from my own family. I feel as if my own flesh and blood share such a blinkered and uncaring attitude towards my diagnosis of PTSD. Maybe I am wrong in thinking this way? But I have only come to this conclusion from the circumstances that have transpired over these past few years.

My twin sister suffers from mental health too, except as far as I know, she does not endure any of the emotional abuse from our family that I have encountered. I have been ostracized, and yet I have never verbally abused any member of my family or shared my views/opinions. I will NOT be silenced; I will NOT refrain from expressing my thoughts; I will NOT allow others to punish me due to their own insecurities. I will live my life my way, on my terms and I DESERVE my children.

Perhaps people like my own family, and some of my extended family, and individuals in the area that I live, should put themselves into the shoes of others and try to comprehend what it must be like to live life with a mental health condition. But in order to do this, each individual needs to understand what compassion, love and empathy is in order to realise what the repercussions of their behaviours and actions will have on those they love or were once acquainted with.

World Health Organisation:

Statistics on Suicide (Aug 2017)

❖ 800,000 people per year take their own life. That equates to one person every 40 seconds.

❖ Second leading cause of death among 15-29 year olds globally in 2015.

❖ For every suicide there are many more people who attempt suicide every year. A prior suicide attempt is the single most important risk factor for suicide in the general population.

❖ Suicide does not occur in high-income countries, but is a global phenomenon in all regions of the World.

❖ 78% of global suicides occurred in low-and middle-income countries 2015.

❖ The effects of suicide are widespread across families, communities and entire countries and has long-lasting effects on the people who are left behind.

❖ Suicides accounted for 1.4% of all deaths worldwide making it the 17th leading cause of death in 2015.

❖ Effective evidence-based interventions can be implemented at population, sub-population and individual levels to prevent suicide and suicide attempts.

❖ Ingestion of pesticides, hanging, and firearms are among the most common methods of suicide globally.

❖ Suicide is a serious public health problem; however, suicides are preventable with timely, evidence-based and often low-cost interventions. For national responses to be effective, a comprehensive multi-sectoral suicide prevention strategy is needed.

(Please note: all information/statistics correct at time of publishing)

Who is at risk?

Whilst the link between suicide and mental disorders (in particular, depression and alcohol-use disorders) is well established in high-income countries, many suicides happen impulsively in moments of crisis. These moments are brought on by a breakdown in the ability to deal with life stresses, such as financial problems, relationship break-up or chronic pain and illness.

WHAT DO I LOVE DOING?

WHAT MAKES ME HAPPY?

CHAPTER 9
THE ART OF BONDING

Blurred Vision

Blurred vision through my windscreen

Whilst driving in the rain

Will my life choices become clearer?

Can I wipe away the pain?

Lights flashing, indicator ticking

My car's about to take a turn

Should I go left or right?

From this choice, I might just learn

That no matter what direction you go

The journey may be filled with stress

But just embrace what's lies ahead

For all we can do is try our best

To take the right path would be rewarding

Our new life we could create

Devoid of toxic twists 'n' turns

Now wouldn't that feel great!

I felt the need to start this chapter with a poem I wrote recently whilst sitting in my car. My day was wrought with stress and unhappiness, so I decided to go for a drive to clear my head and come to terms with my thoughts. It was due to a combination of difficult events which led to my decision to get in my car. My mindset was that the passage of time would help me to find some answers to some very difficult and traumatic life experiences that I have witnessed over the course of many years. Such traumatic events range from a troubled childhood; a controlling upbringing; the death of loved ones, especially my beloved son; an abusive marriage; disownment from my own family; diagnosis of PTSD; losing custody of my 5 children.

What does the word 'relationship' mean to you? To me it means a connection, a bond with another human being that is filled with mutual love, respect and understanding. Yet sadly, in many cases, this is so far from the truth. A dark truth which can have a profound effect on us throughout our lifetime.

Oxford Dictionary meaning – Relationship; The way in which two or more people or things are connected, or the state of being connected.

There are many relationships that evolve in our lifetime:

- Between parents and children

- Between siblings

- Between extended family

- Between friends

- Between co-workers

- Between couples

- Between yourself and your pet(s)

- Between yourself and your possessions

Examples of Symbiosis

Symbiosis is a relationship between two or more organisms that live closely together. Symbiosis comes from two Greek words that mean "with" and "living". There are several types or classes of symbiosis:

Commensalism:

One organism benefits and the other is neither harmed nor helped.

Mutualism:

Both organisms benefit. An obligate mutualist cannot survive without its partner; a facultative mutualist can survive on its own.

Parasitism:

One organism (the parasite) benefits and the other (the host) is harmed.

To be successful, a symbiotic relationship requires a great deal of balance. Even parasitism, where one partner is harmed, the balance is formed so that the host lives long enough to allow the parasite to spread and reproduce. These different forms of symbiosis relate to our everyday life – as a parent; spouse; co-workers or friends. It is inherent within us, within our own unique genetic code, who we choose to be or become. But along the way, the relationships we form with other human beings can either have a positive or negative effect.

MY VERY OWN SYMBIOTIC RELATIONSHIPS

1. Mutualism (both organisms benefit)

2. Commensalism (one organism benefits – neither is harmed or helped)

3. Parasitic (one organism benefits/the other is harmed)

I have come to realise over the years that there is only one person you can rely on in life, and that is yourself. I believe that some individuals mean well by their actions, but only if they are to gain from it. The harsh reality is that many human beings are selfish, greedy, self-centred, and materialistic. People think that you 'give to receive', and an act of kindness should be reciprocated in the same manner. Everyone on this planet has their own reasons as to why they live their life the way they do and the opinions they share. What seems right and just for one person can be a contradiction in terms to another. For who are we to say what it right and wrong in any given situation or circumstance if we have not endured or been witness to certain events in life.

As you have read throughout this book, my life has proved to be a rollercoaster of events and emotions. A rollercoaster which is free to ride yet comes at a price. If someone told me 21 years ago that I would suffer the terrible and tragic loss of one of my children I would not have believed them. For any parent to incur such a huge void in their life turns your world upside down. You have a different outlook on life - who you are and what aspects of it are truly meaningful. Problems that you would have normally seen as 'huge' will seem 'small' in comparison to how you once approached them.

If suffering the loss of my beloved son was not debilitating and heart-breaking enough, as you have read, I am also a survivor of domestic abuse. Since the age of 24 until the present day, my personality has evolved and changed in a myriad of ways and created the person I am today. I've learnt a lot about human nature with regards to how they behave in the face of adversity; how your family can become your own worst enemy; endure financial hardship; face hostility at the school gates; become diagnosed with Post Traumatic Stress Disorder and also the onset of Fibromyalgia; set up my own bone marrow donor appeal on an international level for my beloved son; worked in many different sectors; become a writer for an online magazine and also an aspiring actress; learned how to live without my children full-time. Phew, that's a list! Past events have taken their toll on my mental and physical well-being, and I have become sensible enough to understand that I need to listen to my body more often and seek rest and inner calm when the need dictates.

I am and always will be stunned and shocked by the behaviours of those closest to me over the years. To show such ignorance and hostility is unforgiveable. How does anyone on this planet have the right to treat another human being with such a cold heart? Especially when that individual is related to you. I have lost everything over the years and ended up alone in a one bed flat, at times with little money or love. Who was knocking on my door? Was it those in question whom are related to me by blood? Who comforted me on my beloved son's birthday or anniversary of his passing? Who just popped round for a cup of tea and a hug of support at a time when I needed them the most? I was lost in a cold, heartless world which was filled with warmth and love by my five children.

It's no easy task enduring the explosion of events that I have without the support and help of your own family being by your side, helping you to fight your corner. Yet, I have found an inner strength and determination that I never knew I had. Perhaps fate decided that I needed to become acquainted with these experiences in order for me to come out of my childhood shell and turn the timid, terrified, little girl into the confident, independent, head-strong woman that I am today!

I have spent that past three years fighting for custody of my 4 children and not once did I ever give up on my quest for what I thought was right. At the time of writing this chapter, I am absolutely ecstatic to say that my perseverance and determination has paid off! At long last, my beautiful four children have finally been handed over to me by my ex-husband. Patience and belief in yourself are qualities that keep us alive, that keep us plodding along with our daily routines, in the hope that, in the future, we will reap the rewards of all our efforts.

So here my next journey begins! A full-time mum again to two teenage boys, my daughter and my youngest son. I love all my children equally and respect the fact that they all have different personalities and opinions. Even if they don't know it yet, they are the sole reason I have achieved what I have over the years and evolved into the woman I am now. For my beautiful children have given me love, hope, laughter and hugs since the day that they were born. A mother's love for her child is unconditional and even though the umbilical cord gets cut after birth – emotionally, the cords of our heart strings will always be attached.

For those individuals who have caused me pain due to their own weaknesses and insecurity and have failed to show solidarity to a bereaved, abused woman - all I can say is that I feel sorry for you. Sorry that you do not possess the inner strength and courage that I now do. Perhaps, if there is one thing that you would like to change in your lifetime, perhaps it should be your attitude towards people who have suffered in a way you have never experienced. It is all too easy to express opinions based upon only limited facts, yet no opinion should ever be expressed without knowledge of all the facts and evidence. Never try to judge another human being if you have not walked in their shoes.

'Courage is what it takes to stand up and speak. Courage is also what it takes to sit down and listen'.

Sir Winston Churchill.

I have loved, I have lost and I have learnt. I will always strive to be the best that I can be. I have grown invisible wings and learnt how to fly, and oh my goodness, it feels so good!

Connect with me:

www.onevoicemychoice.co.uk

www.starnow.co.uk

Facebook: Donna Anne Pace

Twitter: @OneVoice2020

Instagram: @onevoicemychoice

LinkedIn: Donna Anne Pace

ACKNOWLEDGEMENTS

His Holiness, Dalai Lama

Buddha

Usain Bolt – Olympic Legend

The Late-Sir Winston Churchill (1874-1965)

The Missing Piece Magazine & Book Series, Kate Batten

The Late-Edmond Locard (1877-1966)

The Late-Nathaniel Branden - (1913-2014)

World Health Organisation

Anthony Nolan Charity

Rethink.org

Victor Vella, Journalist, Malta

Maltese Culture Movement Club

Maltese Prime Minister's Private Secretary

The Royal Bank of Scotland

Major news networks; radio stations; local & national newspapers and magazines.

'Broken' produced by A&SK Films

The first book in The Reinvention Series

The Reinvention of Me

The Second book in The Reinvention Series

Giving Women A Voice - available on Amazon Spring 2020

The Reinvention of Me

Printed in Great Britain
by Amazon